JOB

A Good Man Asks
Why

A Guided Discovery for Groups and Individuals

Kevin Perrotta

LOYOLAPRESS.

CHICAGO

LOYOLAPRESS.

3441 N. ASHLAND AVENUE
CHICAGO, ILLINOIS 60657

Nihil Obstat	*Imprimatur*
Reverend Michael Mulhall, O.Carm.	Most Reverend Raymond E. Goedert,
Censor Deputatus	M.A., S.T.L., J.C.L.
February 29, 2000	Vicar General
	Archdiocese of Chicago
	February 29, 2000

The *Nihil Obstat* and *Imprimatur* are official declarations that a book is free of doctrinal and moral error. No implication is contained therein that those who have granted the *Nihil Obstat* and *Imprimatur* agree with the content, opinions, or statements expressed.

The Scripture quotations contained herein are from the New Revised Standard Version Bible: Catholic Edition, copyright © 1993 and 1989 by the Division of Christian Education of the National Council of the Churches of Christ in the U.S.A. Used by permission. All rights reserved. Subheadings in Scripture quotations have been added by Kevin Perrotta.

The Latin text of St. Augustine's *Confessions* (p. 18) may be found in Pierre de Labriolle, *Saint Augustin: Confessions* (Paris: Société d'Edition "Les Belles Lettres," 1926). Translation by Kevin Perrotta.

The Latin text of Thomas Aquinas's comments on Job (p. 19) may be found in *Divi Thomae Aquinatis Expositio in Job* (Naples: Typographia Virgiliana, 1857). Translation by Kevin Perrotta.

Lourdie Sanon's prayer (p. 29) is reprinted from Louise Perrotta, *All You Really Need to Know about Prayer You Can Learn from the Poor* (Ann Arbor, Mich.: Charis Books, 1996); © 1996 Food for The Poor.

The prayer of Mother Teresa of Calcutta (p. 38) is from her book, *A Gift for God: Prayers and Meditations* (New York: HarperSanFrancisco, 1996).

The French text of Marguerite-Marie Teilhard de Chardin's prayer (p. 39) may be found in her book, *L'Energie spirituelle de la souffrance* (Paris: Editions du Seuil, 1951). Translation by Louise Perrotta.

The comment by Benedict J. Groeschel, C.F.R., (p. 39) is from his book *Stumbling Blocks or Stepping Stones* (New York: Paulist Press, 1987).

The letter of Jane de Chantal (p. 49) may be found in Péronne Marie Thibert, V.H.M., trans., *Francis de Sales, Jane de Chantal: Letters of Spiritual Direction* (New York: Paulist Press, 1988); © 1988 Péronne Marie Thibert, V.H.M., Wendy M. Wright, Joseph Power, O.S.F.S.

The full prayer of John Henry Newman (p. 58) may be found in *Meditations and Devotions* (London, New York: Longmans, Green, 1954).

The Latin text of the excerpt from Gregory the Great (p. 59) may be found in *S. Gregorii Magni Moralia in Job, Libri XXIII–XXXV,* Corpus Christianorum, Series Latina, vol. 143B (Turnholt: Typographi Brepols, 1985). Translation by Kevin Perrotta.

John Paul II's reflections *On the Christian Meaning of Suffering* may be purchased from the National Conference of Catholic Bishops (800) 235-8722.

Interior design by Kay Hartmann/Communique Design
Illustration by Charise Mericle Harper

ISBN 0-8294-1446-0

Printed in the United States of America

02 03 04 05 06 Bang 7 6 5 4 3

Contents

How to Use This Guide

You might compare this booklet to a short visit to a national park. The park is so large that you could spend months, even years, getting to know it. But a brief visit, if carefully planned, can be enjoyable and worthwhile. In a few hours you can drive through the park and pull over at a handful of sites. At each stop you can get out of the car, take a short trail through the woods, listen to the wind blowing in the trees, get a feel for the place.

In this booklet we'll drive through the book of Job, making half a dozen stops along the way. At those points we'll proceed on foot, taking a leisurely walk through the selected passages. The readings have been chosen to lead us to the heart of the debate about the meaning of suffering that takes place in the book of Job. After each discussion we'll get back in the car and take the highway to the next stop.

This guide provides everything you need to explore Job in six discussions—or to do a six-part exploration on your own. The introduction on page 6 will prepare you to get the most out of your reading. The weekly sections feature key passages from Job, with explanations that highlight what his words mean for us today. Equally important, each section supplies questions that will launch you into fruitful discussion, helping you both to explore Job for yourself and to learn from one another. If you're using the booklet by yourself, the questions will spur your personal reflection.

Each discussion is meant to be a *guided discovery.*

Guided. None of us is equipped to read the Bible without help. We read the Bible *for* ourselves but not *by* ourselves. Scripture was written to be understood and applied in and with the Church. So each week "A Guide to the Reading," drawing on the work of both modern biblical scholars and Christian writers of the past, supplies background and explanations. The guide will help you grasp Job's message. Think of it as a friendly park ranger who points out noteworthy details and explains what you're looking at so you can appreciate things for yourself.

Discovery. The purpose is for *you* to interact with the book of Job. "Questions for Careful Reading" is a tool to help you dig into the book and examine it carefully. "Questions for Application" will help you consider what it means for your life here and now. Each week concludes with an "Approach to Prayer" section that helps you respond to God's Word. Supplementary "Living Tradition" and "Saints in the Making" sections offer the thoughts, experiences, and prayers of Christians past and present in order to show you what Job has meant to others—so that you can consider what it might mean for you.

How long are the discussion sessions? We've assumed you will have about an hour and a half when you get together. If you have less time, you'll find that most of the elements can be shortened somewhat.

Is homework necessary? You will get the most out of the discussions if you read the weekly material in advance of each meeting. But if participants are not able to prepare, have someone read the "What's Happened" and "Guide to the Reading" sections aloud to the group at the points where they occur in the weekly material.

What about leadership? If you happen to have a world-class biblical scholar in your group, by all means ask him or her to lead the discussions. But in the absence of any professional Scripture scholars, or even accomplished biblical amateurs, you can still have a first-class Bible discussion. Choose two or three people to be facilitators, and have everyone read "Suggestions for Bible Discussion Groups" before beginning (page 76).

Does everyone need a guide? a Bible? Everyone in the group will need their own copy of this booklet. It contains the sections of Job that are discussed, so a Bible is not absolutely necessary—but each participant will find it useful to have one. You should have at least one Bible on hand for your discussion. (See page 80 for recommendations.)

How do we get started? Before you begin, take a look at the suggestions for Bible discussion groups (page 76) and individuals (page 79).

A Book That Asks Hard Questions

Introducing the Book of Job

To start you thinking about the subject of the book of Job, I was going to begin this introduction with a story or two about people who are suffering. But is there any need? We are all well-acquainted with situations of pain and loss, including the kind that the book of Job portrays, in which the suffering seems undeserved, even terribly unfair. If the starting point for reading Job is an awareness of suffering, we all, sadly, have plenty of material to begin.

Sooner or later, pain draws from us the agonizing question *Why?* Why has God let this dreadful thing happen to me or to another person? Why has God created a universe where such suffering can occur? How can God be just—indeed, how can God *be*—if such evil exists? What possible use can this suffering serve?

To some people it may appear that such questions are inappropriate for a person of faith. The person who asks them may seem to lack trust in God. The questions may even seem dangerous, for often they are asked with anger, and it may seem unwise to get angry with God. And what if the questions have no good answers? In that case, it might be better not to pursue them, since they would only undermine our faith.

The biblical, Christian tradition, however, does not counsel timidity or repression in our relationship with the Almighty. The writers of Scripture and the saints of the Church model honesty with God. Faith does not entail weak-minded avoidance of hard questions. Asking questions, even with deep feeling, is a necessary part of progress toward the truth. God is not afraid of our questions; in fact, he welcomes them. Concerning the *why?* that we cry out in suffering, Pope John Paul II has written: "Man can put this question to God with all the emotion of his heart and with his mind full of dismay and anxiety, and God expects the question and listens to it, as we see in the revelation of the Old Testament. In the book of Job the question has found its most vivid expression."

The Pope sounds almost like he is writing the introduction to this booklet. The book of Job is indeed the Bible's most vivid and profound examination of the meaning of human suffering. Reading Job will lead us to reflect on our own questions about God and suffering—a process of reflection that can help us to mature in faith. Job will also spur us to reflect on less theoretical questions—how suffering should be borne, how comfort to the suffering should (and should not) be given, how comfort should be received.

The central question. Probably all people who have suffered, whatever their beliefs about God or gods, have asked why. The Jewish and Christian view of God gives the question a special urgency. The God who made himself known to Israel and revealed himself perfectly in Jesus of Nazareth is the creator and ruler of all. He is a just and loving God who takes a deep interest in human beings and promises to lead us into happiness with himself. The evils that arise in the world force us to ask how *this* God, who is so powerful and so compassionate, can allow so much to happen that seems to contradict his purposes.

For some people, this question takes the form of what has been called "the problem of pain." The question is whether the existence of a powerful and loving God who is deeply involved in human lives can be squared with the existence of extreme suffering. Some people reason that an all-powerful and perfectly loving God would not allow great evils to occur; since there are great evils in the world, either God does not exist or, contrary to Jewish and Christian belief, he is not all-powerful or all-loving or deeply involved in our lives.

This "problem of pain" reflects a modern way of thinking. In ancient cultures, it was impossible to imagine the kind of atheism that the problem of pain leads some people to embrace today. To the ancient Israelites in the centuries before Christ, the question about God and suffering was this: Given that God *is* powerful and just, can we interpret suffering as an expression of God's administration of justice? That is to say, is *all* suffering God's punishment, or at least his discipline, for sin?

In ancient Israel, many people would answer yes to this question. The author of Job, however, disagreed, and he undertook to write a story that would demonstrate the inadequacy of that answer and explore whether there is an alternative explanation. For the sake of argument, the author supposed that there was once a thoroughly upright person, a person who, at least in every important way, did exactly what God wanted—a person who did not need punishment or correction. What if this person were afflicted by great evils? To develop his idea, the author, it seems, adapted a legend about a figure named Job (he is mentioned elsewhere in the Bible, in a way that assumes that readers are familiar with the legend—Ezekiel 14:14, 20). Job is a good man who suffers grievous losses and is struck with a loathsome disease.

The author expands the legend into a lengthy consideration of the meaning of suffering. For the bulk of the book, Job and some of his friends engage in a debate. The friends defend the traditional view that suffering is God's punishment or discipline for sin. Job, who used to accept this view, now angrily rejects it, because it no longer fits his experience. Job expresses rage and confusion, a desire for justice and a longing for death, trust in God and disappointment with God. The friends, applying the traditional explanation of suffering to Job's situation, conclude that he has committed some grave sin. Insisting that he has *not* sinned, at least not in any serious way, Job seeks a confrontation with God—a kind of day in court in which he can vindicate his innocence. By implication, Job's vindication would mean that God has dealt unfairly with him. Finally God appears and speaks. God rebukes Job—but then rebukes Job's friends even more severely!

This nutshell summary of the book hardly does it justice. The conversation between Job and the friends, for example, is not a straightforward debate. To a great extent the friends and Job talk past each other; the friends do not come to grips with Job's situation, and he must struggle with the apparent injustice of his suffering alone. Job's isolation is, in fact, accentuated by the presence of friends who do not really understand him. With moving poetry Job bemoans the fragility and brevity of human life (chapter 14) and recalls with sorrow his happier days (chapter 29). He berates his unsympathetic friends (6:14–21; 12:1–6; 13:1–5; 16:1–6). He declares the inaccessibility of true wisdom (chapter 28). He shrieks with protest against God's blows (chapters 7, 10), yet paradoxically he trusts in God's goodness; with seeming illogic, he even relies on God to defend him against God who is unjustly afflicting him (16:11–22; 19:8–22, 25–27). Such passages give this book a complexity, depth, and beauty that place it on a par with other literary masterpieces probing the existence of evil in the world, such as St. Augustine's *City of God,* Shakespeare's *King Lear,* and Milton's *Paradise Lost.* Even if the book of Job were not God's inspired word, it would deserve our attention as a profound examination of the human condition.

In this booklet we will not try to investigate the book of Job in all its complexity. We will simply follow the main thread of the argument, leaving much else aside. This approach is actually a good way to read Job for the first time. Once you are familiar with the main road, you are better able to explore the side roads without getting lost. If you would like to go beyond the sections of Job that we read here, you might look at the sections mentioned in parentheses in the preceding paragraph. Then go back to the beginning and read the whole book all the way through, preferably with the help of a study Bible or commentary (see page 80).

Where Job leaves us. The book of Job completes a stage in the human journey toward an understanding of suffering. Job clears away a false interpretation—often a necessary step in attaining the truth—and opens the way to a better explanation. But the book of Job does not offer a better explanation. The book leaves us with a humble awareness of the limitations on our ability to grasp the mystery of suffering. If we are to understand more, we will need God to shed more light on the subject. An article at the end of this booklet explores how God has done this through his Son's becoming a human being and sharing our suffering. Along the way, the "Saints in the Making" and "Living Tradition" pieces feature thoughts and prayers on suffering from the perspective of faith in Christ.

CRUSHED IN THE PRIME OF LIFE

Questions to Begin

15 minutes
Use a question or two to get warmed up for the reading.

---

1 When you were a teenager and went out at night, your parents would
❑ enjoy having a little peace and quiet.
❑ assume you were getting into trouble.
❑ forget you were out.
❑ pray the rosary.
❑ wait up for you.
❑ wait up awhile, then go to bed.
❑ start calling your friends' parents if you didn't come in on time.
❑ grill you afterwards about where you were, who you were with, what you were doing.

---

2 What do you think "fear of the Lord" means? Do you "fear the Lord"? Why or why not?

5 minutes
Read the passage aloud. Let individuals take turns reading sections.

The Reading: Job 1:1–2:10

God Tests Job

1 There was once a man in the land of Uz whose name was Job. That man was blameless and upright, one who feared God and turned away from evil. 2 There were born to him seven sons and three daughters. 3 He had seven thousand sheep, three thousand camels, five hundred yoke of oxen, five hundred donkeys, and very many servants; so that this man was the greatest of all the people of the east. 4 His sons used to go and hold feasts in one another's houses in turn; and they would send and invite their three sisters to eat and drink with them. 5 And when the feast days had run their course, Job would send and sanctify them, and he would rise early in the morning and offer burnt offerings according to the number of them all; for Job said, "It may be that my children have sinned, and cursed God in their hearts." This is what Job always did.

6 One day the heavenly beings came to present themselves before the LORD, and Satan* also came among them. 7 The LORD said to Satan, "Where have you come from?" Satan answered the LORD, "From going to and fro on the earth, and from walking up and down on it." 8 The LORD said to Satan, "Have you considered my servant Job? There is no one like him on the earth, a blameless and upright man who fears God and turns away from evil." 9 Then Satan answered the LORD, "Does Job fear God for nothing? 10 Have you not put a fence around him and his house and all that he has, on every side? You have blessed the work of his hands, and his possessions have increased in the land. 11 But stretch out your hand now, and touch all that he has, and he will curse you to your face." 12 The LORD said to Satan, "Very well, all that he has is in your power; only do not stretch out your hand against him!" So Satan went out from the presence of the LORD.

13 One day when his sons and daughters were eating and drinking wine in the eldest brother's house, 14 a messenger came to Job and said, "The oxen were plowing and the donkeys were feeding beside them, 15 and the Sabeans fell on them and carried them off,

* Literally "the Accuser"

and killed the servants with the edge of the sword; I alone have escaped to tell you." 16 While he was still speaking, another came and said, "The fire of God fell from heaven and burned up the sheep and the servants, and consumed them; I alone have escaped to tell you." 17 While he was still speaking, another came and said, "The Chaldeans formed three columns, made a raid on the camels and carried them off, and killed the servants with the edge of the sword; I alone have escaped to tell you." 18 While he was still speaking, another came and said, "Your sons and daughters were eating and drinking wine in their eldest brother's house, 19 and suddenly a great wind came across the desert, struck the four corners of the house, and it fell on the young people, and they are dead; I alone have escaped to tell you."

20 Then Job arose, tore his robe, shaved his head, and fell on the ground and worshiped. 21 He said, "Naked I came from my mother's womb, and naked shall I return there; the LORD gave, and the LORD has taken away; blessed be the name of the LORD."

22 In all this Job did not sin or charge God with wrongdoing.

The Test Gets Harder

2:1 One day the heavenly beings came to present themselves before the LORD, and Satan also came among them to present himself before the LORD. . . . 3 The LORD said to Satan, "Have you considered my servant Job? There is no one like him on the earth, a blameless and upright man who fears God and turns away from evil. He still persists in his integrity, although you incited me against him, to destroy him for no reason." 4 Then Satan answered the LORD, "Skin for skin! All that people have they will give to save their lives. 5 But stretch out your hand now and touch his bone and his flesh, and he will curse you to your face." 6 The LORD said to Satan, "Very well, he is in your power; only spare his life."

7 So Satan went out from the presence of the LORD, and inflicted loathsome sores on Job from the sole of his foot to the crown of his head. 8 Job took a potsherd with which to scrape himself, and sat among the ashes.

9 Then his wife said to him, "Do you still persist in your integrity? Curse God, and die." 10 But he said to her, "You speak as any foolish woman would speak. Shall we receive the good at the hand of God, and not receive the bad?" In all this Job did not sin with his lips.

Questions for Careful Reading

10 minutes
Choose questions according to your interest and time.

1 Locate the verses in which Job speaks. What impression of him do you get simply from his own words?

2 Why does God allow Satan to afflict Job?

3 Job's children perish while they are feasting—the very situation in which Job tried to protect them by his prayers. What message might there be in this?

4 What is a potsherd? Why would a person want to scrape tender sores?

5 What would the disasters that befell Job have meant for his wife?

A Guide to the Reading

If participants have not read this section already, read it aloud. Otherwise go on to "Questions for Application."

The Hebrew text begins vaguely: "A man there was" (1:1), like the opening of a parable ("A man had two sons"). The author says nothing about the man's background, only that he lives in "the land of Uz" (1:1), a perhaps legendary place, somewhere in the East. A man of indistinct origins, Job is an everyman, a person with whom anyone could identify.

Job possesses oxen for farming, sheep for pasturing, camels for trading, and servants for running a large household (1:3). In those days men and women married in their teens, but Job's daughters, at least, appear to be unmarried, so they must be quite young, and Job himself not old. He is a wealthy, busy, middle-aged man with a lot to live for.

Most important, Job is good. The author makes this point four times over (1:1); God himself declares it proudly (1:8). Job's goodness, it is later seen, lies in his justice, compassion, and generosity (29:11–17; 31:1–40). He does more than God requires, offering sacrifices even for sins that may not have been committed (1:5). Job's goodness is a polestar that we must keep in view as we navigate through the story ahead.

Ancient readers would not have been surprised that upright Job was also affluent. They regarded morality and prosperity as a package: live right and God will bless you. Job accepted this traditional view, and so did the original readers. It is a view, perhaps unexamined, held by many of us today. The book of Job will help us examine it.

The next character to appear, God, is pictured as an ancient Near Eastern king sitting on a throne with attendants and government ministers standing around him (1:6). Among his servants is "Satan" (1:6). Significantly, in the Hebrew he is called *"the* Satan." "Satan" is not his personal name but his office. He is "the accuser, the opponent," a royal agent who investigates and prosecutes antigovernment activities. Jewish and Christian tradition later adopted "Satan" as the personal name of the prince of devils (see Revelation 12:9–10). In Job, however, "the Satan" is a functionary in the heavenly court. Job is a story, not a theological treatise; consequently the heavenly court and the Satan are imaginative devices for creating a narrative, rather than literal features of heaven.

As God-the-king's servant, even if a somewhat unpleasant one, the Satan has the royal interests in mind. It is his duty to point out possible disloyalty. He is a kind of "devil's advocate." The Satan does not deny that Job is pious, but he alleges that his piety is less than wholehearted (1:9–11). Granted that Job is an upright person; but *why* does he do right? Is it because he loves God—or because he loves the good things that God gives him? The Satan claims that Job's devotion to God is not as deep as it appears. If God were to remove his blessings, Job would "charge God with wrongdoing" (1:22), that is, he would accuse God of being unjust.

God decides to test Job, as he once tested Abraham (see Genesis 22), to get at the truth about him. The only way to find out if Job serves God only because of the good things that God gives him is to take the good things away. So God commissions the Satan to do that. The Satan inflicts the disasters, but only as God's agent; God is responsible for what befalls Job (2:3). This immediately suggests that the traditional doctrine—God always rewards good behavior in this world—does not provide a comprehensive explanation for all of God's dealings with people.

Disasters come in rapid succession, leaving Job no time to react until the whole series of calamities has been announced (1:13–19). Then he bows to the ground—an expression of both worship and prostration under the load of woes (1:20). His first words are to bless God (1:21). To "bless" God is to declare that God is the source of good things. Job continues to acknowledge God as giver, even when his gifts are withdrawn. Job has passed the test.

In a second conference, God acknowledges that he has afflicted Job "for no reason" (2:3), that is, even though Job did not deserve it. He then mandates a second round of testing (2:6).

Job's wife advises him to accuse God of wrongdoing and bring down divine wrath on himself: suicide by blasphemy (2:9). Job, however, steadfastly says only what is right about God (2:10). But will he continue to do so?

Questions for Application

40 minutes
Choose questions according to your interest and time.

1 God considers the Satan's question important—so important that it warrants subjecting Job to testing in order to determine the answer. Why is the question important?

2 What are your motivations for obeying God? In what ways are your motivations mixed? What are good and not-so-good reasons for obeying God? What effect do a person's motivations have on their relationship with God?

3 Job tries to preserve his children's relationship with God and protect them from harm. How attainable are these goals by parents? What can parents do for their children spiritually? What can't parents do? What should they not try to do? To what degree do the answers depend on children's ages?

4 In what ways do spouses affect each other's attitudes and behavior? How do spouses sometimes discourage each other? How can spouses encourage each other?

5 When has suffering or loss broken in on you unexpectedly during a time of happiness and peace? How did you react? What did you learn from this experience? How has it affected your relationship with God?

"Try to curb any natural tendency to either excessive talking or excessive quiet. You and the rest of the group will benefit."

Christian Basics Bible Studies series, InterVarsity Press

Approach to Prayer

15 minutes
Use this approach—or create your own!

✦ Reflect on the difference between loving God and loving the things that God gives. Let one person read aloud this prayer from St. Augustine's *Confessions.* After a few minutes of silence, pray an Our Father aloud together.

Late, late have I loved you, Beauty so old and so new! Here you were within me, and I was outside, searching for you there, blundering disgracefully among the lovely things you have made. You were with me, but I was not with you. Things that would not have existed apart from you kept me apart from you. You called and shouted and broke through my deafness. You flashed and shone and pierced my blindness. You blazed with ardor, and I breathed in your fragrance, and now I pant for you. You touched me, and I burn with longing for your peace.

A Living Tradition

A Perceptive Reader

This section is a supplement for individual reading.

Thomas Aquinas, a great theologian who lived in the thirteenth century, was a perceptive reader of the Bible. Here are a few remarks that St. Thomas made on Job.

On the sequence of Job's woes (1:13–19; 2:7).
First the loss of his property is reported, second the crushing of his offspring, third his own personal torment. This progression is for the purpose of increasing his suffering, for a person who has been crushed by a greater misfortune does not feel a lesser one; but after a lesser misfortune, the person feels a greater one. Therefore, so that Job might feel the particular suffering of each misfortune, Satan began to afflict him with a lesser misfortune and proceeded little by little to the greater.

On the timing of his children's death (1:13, 18).
It is likely that a dinner party in the house of the first-born son would be particularly festive. It is worth considering that people are more shaken by things that happen to them suddenly, for misfortunes foreseen are more easily endured. In order, then, that Job might be shaken, Satan brought misfortune on him at a very pleasant time, when he was less able to think about misfortune. Thus the very presence of enjoyment would make the misfortune seem heavier.

On the meaning of Satan's obscure statement: "Skin for skin! All that people have they will give to save their lives" (2:4). "Skin for skin," that is, "someone else's flesh for his own." For a man who is not virtuous will bear up when others, even those who are close to him, suffer rather than himself. Any man will give everything external in order to save his life.

Thomas, it seems, thinks that Job refrained from expressing anger toward God when his children died because he feared that God would punish such an outburst by inflicting physical suffering on him. Thus, Satan alleges, Job saved his own skin by maintaining a prudent silence when his children lost their lives. Thomas writes, "Satan means that Job endured the loss of his possessions and his children patiently for the safety of his own body. Satan points out that this was not very virtuous behavior, since it was only human."

A CRY OF PAIN

Questions to Begin

15 minutes
Use a question or two to get warmed up for the reading.

1 When have you expressed a deep feeling or conviction through something you built, made, wrote, painted, performed, or designed?

2 What was the hardest day of your life? What happened?

3 What are some ways that you comfort friends when they experience a loss?

5 minutes
Read the passage aloud. Let individuals take turns reading sections.

The Reading: Job 2:11–3:26

Friends Assemble

11 Now when Job's three friends heard of all these troubles that had come upon him, each of them set out from his home—Eliphaz the Temanite, Bildad the Shuhite, and Zophar the Naamathite. They met together to go and console and comfort him. 12 When they saw him from a distance, they did not recognize him, and they raised their voices and wept aloud; they tore their robes and threw dust in the air upon their heads. 13 They sat with him on the ground seven days and seven nights, and no one spoke a word to him, for they saw that his suffering was very great.

Job Curses His Beginnings

3:1 After this Job opened his mouth and cursed the day of his birth.
2 Job said:
> 3 "Let the day perish in which I was born,
>> and the night that said,
>> 'A man-child is conceived.'
> 4 Let that day be darkness!
>> May God above not seek it,
>> or light shine on it.
> 5 Let gloom and deep darkness claim it.
>> Let clouds settle upon it;
>> let the blackness of the day terrify it.
> 6 That night—let thick darkness seize it!
>> let it not rejoice among the days of the year;
>> let it not come into the number of the months.
> 7 Yes, let that night be barren;
>> let no joyful cry be heard in it. . . .
> 9 Let the stars of its dawn be dark;
>> let it hope for light, but have none;
>> may it not see the eyelids of the morning—
> 10 because it did not shut the doors of my mother's womb,
>> and hide trouble from my eyes."

Job Longs for Death

11 "Why did I not die at birth,
   come forth from the womb and expire?
12 Why were there knees to receive me,
   or breasts for me to suck?
13 Now I would be lying down and quiet;
   I would be asleep; then I would be at rest
14 with kings and counselors of the earth
   who rebuild ruins for themselves,
15 or with princes who have gold,
   who fill their houses with silver.
16 Or why was I not buried like a stillborn child,
   like an infant that never sees the light?
17 There the wicked cease from troubling,
   and there the weary are at rest.
18 There the prisoners are at ease together;
   they do not hear the voice of the taskmaster.
19 The small and the great are there,
   and the slaves are free from their masters.

20 "Why is light given to one in misery,
   and life to the bitter in soul,
21 who long for death, but it does not come,
   and dig for it more than for hidden treasures;
22 who rejoice exceedingly,
   and are glad when they find the grave?
23 Why is light given to one who cannot see the way,
   whom God has fenced in?
24 For my sighing comes like my bread,
   and my groanings are poured out like water.
25 Truly the thing that I fear comes upon me,
   and what I dread befalls me.
26 I am not at ease, nor am I quiet;
   I have no rest; but trouble comes."

10 minutes
Choose questions according to your interest and time.

1 Job's friends come to "console and comfort" him (2:11). In this reading, do they accomplish their purpose?

2 Are the friends completely silent?

3 Why might the severity of Job's suffering keep his friends from speaking to him (2:13)?

4 How has Job changed from last week's reading? What has caused the change?

5 When Job asks "why" in 3:11, is he looking for an explanation or seeking to express something besides a question? What about in 3:20 and 3:23?

6 Does Job think that he has done anything to deserve the suffering that has happened to him?

A Guide to the Reading

If participants have not read this section already, read it aloud.
Otherwise go on to "Questions for Application."

It is a familiar phenomenon. A person faces sudden disaster or bereavement with remarkable calm and presence of mind, but when the initial numbness wears off, the full weight of grief seems more than the person can bear. At first Job reacts to catastrophe with exemplary submission to God's will. He even offers his wife some balanced words to moderate her despair (2:10). During the following days or weeks, however, Job's torment shatters his attitude of acceptance.

Job's three friends would have needed some days or weeks to communicate and meet (2:11). By the time they arrive, Job is so deeply ravaged by sickness and sorrow that they do not "recognize him" (2:12). The Hebrew could also mean they do not "greet him." That is, they do not speak to him; instead, they treat him as one who has already died, performing rituals of mourning for him (2:12–13). For seven days—a full period of mourning—the friends sit with him silently, in total sympathy. Their silence will turn out to be the most helpful part of their visit.

Finally, Job breaks the silence with a cry of pain. He hurls a curse at the night of his conception and the day of his birth (3:3–10). Life has become so hateful that Job regrets that he ever came into existence. His wish that the day of his birth be blotted out—"Let that day be darkness!" (3:4)—is a vehement reversal of God's creative "Let there be light" (Genesis 1:3). His wish that the night of his conception be reduced to silence—"let no joyful cry be heard in it" (3:7)—expresses a desire to silence his parents' joyful wedding procession through town and the sound of lovemaking in the bridal chamber.

A curse calls down destruction. But nothing can destroy a day that has passed. Job's curse expresses impotent rage. He follows it with a despairing lament (3:11–26). In Israelite prayer, people describe their suffering to God to move him to act on their behalf (for example, Psalm 22). But Job's lament is simply a cry of pain, without any expectation that God will come to help. Job is powerless and hopeless.

Job declares that if he had died at birth, everything would be fine with him now (3:11–16). Since he did not die then, he longs for death to come soon (3:17–26). At the time the book of Job was written, the general view in Israel was that the dead were reduced to a shadowy existence without hope of resurrection (belief in resurrection developed only gradually in later centuries). Without prospect of life after death, it was almost unheard of for someone to *long* to die. Sufferers longed to recover and go on living. Job's desire to escape his pain by going down into the realm of the dead may have seemed as bizarre to ancient readers as it would seem bizarre to us if a person longed to escape painful memories by becoming a victim of Alzheimer's disease and going to live in a ward for people suffering dementia. Torments have broken Job's spirit. In the Hebrew text, the last word of Job's lament says it all: "trouble" (3:26). Job's world and Job's heart are filled with turmoil.

Notice that Job speaks not only of his own suffering but also of the suffering of others. Job knows of others whose misery makes them long for death (3:20–21). He refers to men and women who are captured and sold as slaves and forced to carry out hard labor under harsh foremen (see 3:18). As the book proceeds, Job will speak mainly about himself; however, his distress is caused not only by the seeming injustice of his own suffering, but also by the unjust suffering that other people undergo. Job sees himself as an example of the larger problem of undeserved suffering in the world. Has Job's fall from prosperity into misery opened his eyes to see others' suffering more clearly?

In his abyss of pain, Job in effect agrees with his wife that it would be better for him to die than go on suffering (2:9). However, he still avoids accusing God of wrongdoing, as she suggested— but avoids it only narrowly. Cursing the day when God gave him life comes close to cursing God himself. Under further stress, will Job slip over the line and declare that God has acted wrongly?

Questions for Application

40 minutes
Choose questions according to your interest and time.

1 Why is a person's response to tragedy sometimes delayed? Has this ever happened to you? How delayed can a person's response to tragedy be?

2 When is a person's silence more comforting than words? Why? Have you ever remained silent when a friend of yours was suffering?

3 What are ways of expressing grief? In times of great loss, is it better to express grief or to maintain your composure? Why?

4 Job expresses his turmoil in a beautifully composed poem. What role can artistic expression (poetry, music, painting) play in dealing with grief?

5 Have there been times when you thought that life is not worth living? If so, how have you dealt with such times? What part does God play in your life at those times?

6 When has your suffering made you more sensitive to the suffering of others?

"The discussion leader has an important task in sharpening the group's emerging insights by giving careful, accurate summaries of the discussions."

John Burke, O.P., *Beginners' Guide to Bible Sharing*

Approach to Prayer

15 minutes
Use this approach—or create your own!

✦ Use Psalm 69 to pray for people
who are suffering greatly. Let
one member of the group read
aloud the first three verses
(69:1–3, NRSV; 69:2–4, NAB).
Then let anyone who wishes
very briefly mention someone
they know, or about whom they
have heard or read, who is in
great pain or sorrow. Then let
someone read aloud Psalm
69:13–18 (NRSV; 69:14–19,
NAB) as a prayer on behalf of
those mentioned. End by praying the Our Father together.

Saints in the Making

Prayer of a Destitute Widow

This section is a supplement for individual reading.

It's me again, Lord.
I know I call on you all the time, but who else can I talk to?
Who else will help me? Who else sees?
You are the only one who knows.

I see other women with their husbands, and I feel lonely
      sometimes.
I feel that I'm very young to have five children and nobody
      to help me out with them.
Well, that's not quite true. I'm grateful that my brother-in-
      law comes by to give me something sometimes. And
      my aunt has taken us in for a while.

But Lord, I'm afraid they'll get tired of us and won't want to
      help anymore. Even if it's family, you can't live off
      other people forever.
You are the only one who knows.

And Lord, I don't know what to do with these kids.
They are hungry sometimes, and I have nothing to feed them.
      I can't send them to school. I can't provide for them,
      because I can't find any work.
And now my oldest son is sick—so sick, with a high fever
      every night. The doctor prescribed some medicine,
      but you know I have no money to buy it.
God, my son has no father but you. You gave this child and
      you are able to heal him. Lord, I love my son. Please
      save him.
You are the only one who knows.

Thank you, Lord, that I can turn to you with my problems
      and that you are always with me.
If I didn't have you, I could never find the strength even to
      get up in the morning. But you help me out.
I have nothing on my own, but you provide everything, Lord.
Because of that, every day is like a miracle to me.

Lourdie Sanon, Port-au-Prince, Haiti

What Kind of Help Is This?

Questions to Begin

15 minutes
Use a question or two to get warmed up for the reading.

1 What was the best piece of advice that anyone ever gave you? How do you know it was good?

2 What was the worst advice that anyone ever gave you?

3 What is the best and the worst advice you ever gave to someone?

5 minutes
Read the passage aloud. Let individuals take turns reading sections.

The Reading: Job 4; 5

An Encouragement to Trust God

4:1 Then Eliphaz the Temanite answered:

2 "If one ventures a word with you, will you be offended?
But who can keep from speaking?
3 See, you have instructed many;
you have strengthened the weak hands.
4 Your words have supported those who were stumbling,
and you have made firm the feeble knees.
5 But now it has come to you, and you are impatient;
it touches you, and you are dismayed.
6 Is not your fear of God your confidence,
and the integrity of your ways your hope?
7 Think now, who that was innocent ever perished?
Or where were the upright cut off? . . ."

Everyone Sins

17 "'Can mortals be righteous before God?
Can human beings be pure before their Maker?
18 Even in his servants he puts no trust,
and his angels he charges with error;
19 how much more those who live in houses of clay,
whose foundation is in the dust,
who are crushed like a moth. . . .'"

Sin Is the Source of Suffering

5:6 "For misery does not come from the earth,
nor does trouble sprout from the ground;
7 but human beings are born to trouble
just as sparks fly upward."

God Executes Justice in the World

8 "As for me, I would seek God,
and to God I would commit my cause.
9 He does great things and unsearchable,

marvelous things without number.
10 He gives rain on the earth
    and sends waters on the fields;
11 he sets on high those who are lowly,
    and those who mourn are lifted to safety.
12 He frustrates the devices of the crafty,
    so that their hands achieve no success.
13 He takes the wise in their own craftiness;
    and the schemes of the wily are brought to a quick end.
14 They meet with darkness in the daytime,
    and grope at noonday as in the night.
15 But he saves the needy from the sword of their mouth,
    from the hand of the mighty.
16 So the poor have hope,
    and injustice shuts its mouth."

Submitting to God's Discipline Brings Happiness

17 "How happy is the one whom God reproves;
    therefore do not despise the discipline of the Almighty.
18 For he wounds, but he binds up;
    he strikes, but his hands heal. . . .
20 In famine he will redeem you from death,
    and in war from the power of the sword.
21 You shall be hidden from the scourge of the tongue,
    and shall not fear destruction when it comes.
22 At destruction and famine you shall laugh,
    and shall not fear the wild animals of the earth.
23 For you shall be in league with the stones of the field,
    and the wild animals shall be at peace with you.
24 You shall know that your tent is safe,
    you shall inspect your fold and miss nothing.
25 You shall know that your descendants will be many,
    and your offspring like the grass of the earth.
26 You shall come to your grave in ripe old age,
    as a shock of grain comes up to the threshing floor in
        its season.
27 See, we have searched this out; it is true.
    Hear, and know it for yourself."

Questions for Careful Reading

10 minutes
Choose questions according to your interest and time.

1 Why does Job's speech, rather than his suffering, spur Eliphaz to speak?

2 What is "it" in 4:5?

3 In 5:20 Eliphaz makes a promise about what God will do for Job. Judging from what Job said in chapter 3, is this what Job wants?

4 How appropriate is Eliphaz's promise in 5:25?

5 What does Eliphaz think is the reason for Job's suffering? What does he think is the solution? Cite particular lines in Eliphaz's speech.

6 Considering what we know about Job from chapter 1 and what Job himself has said about his situation in chapter 3, how on-target is Eliphaz's advice?

A Guide to the Reading

If participants have not read this section already, read it aloud. Otherwise go on to "Questions for Application."

Before Job spoke, his friends shared his sorrow. His lament spoils the harmony. Listening to Job's curses and complaints, the friends notice that something is missing. Job does not acknowledge having done anything to bring his sufferings down on himself. The friends are sure Job must have sinned: why else would such horrible things have happened to him? His lack of remorse, then, impedes his recovery. In today's terminology, Job is in denial. In addition, his failure to acknowledge any wrongdoing implies that God is treating him unfairly. Both as friends of Job and defenders of God, the visitors must protest.

The first to speak, Eliphaz, reminds Job of the traditional view: God rules the world like a benevolent king, rewarding the just, punishing the wicked, helping the needy (4:7; 5:9–16; compare Psalms 34; 37:28–40). Eliphaz reflects on the sources of human sorrows. Troubles come to us not because nature is hostile (5:6) but because of our own bad choices. "Human beings are born to trouble" (5:7), Eliphaz declares; his words might be translated, "human beings *beget* trouble." To adapt Shakespeare, "The fault is not in our stars, dear Job, but in ourselves."

Job's sufferings would seem to disprove Eliphaz's view, since, as Eliphaz recognizes, Job is a man of integrity (4:6). But Eliphaz makes a qualification: no one is *completely* upright (4:17–19). Since everybody sins somewhat, everybody brings some suffering on themselves.

Eliphaz distinguishes between major and minor sinners. There are wicked people, who set themselves stubbornly against God. God brings them to a quick end; he cuts them off in the middle of their natural life span (5:13–14). Then there are upright people like Job. They generally follow God's ways but sometimes go astray. Evils that befall them are a warning to repent, an expression of God's loving discipline. If the upright turn back to God, he restores their fortunes (5:17–18).

Until now Eliphaz and Job have shared this view. On the basis of this common heritage, Eliphaz now tactfully makes an appeal. "You've lived a decent life. Why give up hope now? If you acknowledge your sins, God will set things right for you" (see

4:3–7; 5:17–26). While it may seem that Eliphaz accuses Job of being "offended" and "impatient" (4:2, 5), the Hebrew word used in both instances could also be translated as "weak," "tired," or "discouraged." Eliphaz recognizes Job's exhaustion and chides him gently.

Eliphaz's analysis is very neat. His theory provides a simple explanation for Job's (and everybody else's) suffering and points to an always accessible solution. The severity of Job's suffering, however, should alert Eliphaz to a flaw in his theory of disciplinary pain. Only a moral monster would need such immense losses and revolting sickness to prod him to repentance. Eliphaz should know Job well enough to recognize that Job does not need such ferocious discipline (4:3–6).

But Eliphaz does not acknowledge the depths of Job's pain. He offers a cheery promise of restored life (5:18–26) to a man whose agony makes him long for death (chapter 3). He recites familiar maxims about the punishment of the wicked, which have no relevance to Job, a man of integrity. He offers Job conventional, off-the-rack statements, without considering whether they fit Job at all (5:8–16, 20–21, and especially 25). Eliphaz is full of wise sayings but is not wise enough to know when they apply and when they don't. Eliphaz lacks the compassion of the Samaritan in Jesus' parable: the Samaritan came across a man in pain, and "when he saw him, he was moved with pity" (Luke 10:33). Eliphaz does not seem to see or to pity. He does not realize that Job's suffering is a mystery that he has not figured out.

Job may very well have offered the same sort of view to other sufferers in the past (4:3–4). But his experience has now destroyed his confidence in it. A gap has opened between theory and reality, and Job has fallen into it. Job knows that he has not done anything wrong (we readers know it too), yet he suffers terribly. The traditional view is obviously inadequate.

Job could easily accept Eliphaz's advice: admit that he has committed some sin, go through a ritual of repentance, and wait for God to restore his fortunes. But to agree that his suffering is God's correction would be dishonest, and Job is an honest man. As we will see in our next reading, Job will not play guilty.

Questions for Application

40 minutes
Choose questions according to your interest and time.

1 From your experience of giving and receiving comfort in times of suffering or sorrow, what kind of consolation is truly consoling? What makes it so? How can you know what is helpful to say?

2 When have you been especially comforted in the midst of sorrow? When have you been able to comfort another person? What effect has this had on your life?

3 What makes some attempts to console a suffering person inappropriate? What are the harmful effects of glib advice and pat reasoning?

4 What sorts of things that people sometimes say to the suffering seem designed to comfort the comforter more than the sufferer?

5 When has suffering played a part in helping you come to a deeper commitment to God?

6 Whom do you rely on for advice? How can you tell if you're getting good advice? How can a person choose wise counselors?

7 Eliphaz assumed that Job's sufferings were due to his sins. Explore some situations in which this assumption is applied today to entire groups of people. What are the shortcomings of Eliphaz's reasoning when it is applied to groups, classes, nations, etc.?

In a discussion about the Bible, "periods of silence are reflective moments filled with growth. They should be handled lovingly and carefully."

Loretta Girzaitis, *Guidebook for Bible Study*

Approach to Prayer

15 minutes
Use this approach—or create your own!

✦ Pray for compassion, for avoiding snap judgments about those who suffer, for a spirit of gentleness and patience with those who are in sorrow. Let someone read aloud the following prayer by Mother Teresa of Calcutta.

Dearest Lord, may I see you today and every day in the person of your sick, and, while nursing them, minister unto you. Though you hide yourself behind the unattractive disguise of the irritable, the exacting, the unreasonable, may I still recognize you, and say, "Jesus, my patient, how sweet it is to serve you."

Allow a few minutes for silent prayer and for any spontaneous prayers that anyone wishes to express. End by praying the Our Father together.

Saints in the Making

Prayer of a Chronically Ill Person

This section is a supplement for individual reading.

Lord, the day has just come to an end. Like all the others, it leaves me with an impression of total failure. I have done nothing for you: no prayers that I am aware of, nor any works of charity, nor the slightest bit of work. . . . I have not even been able to control that childish impatience and those stupid grudges that too often usurp your place in the no-man's-land of my feelings. It is in vain that I promise you to do better: tomorrow will probably be no better. . . .

When I look back over the course of my life, I am over-whelmed by the same sense of inadequacy. I have sought you. . . . But as I sought you, wasn't it myself that I was finding and seeking to jus-tify? Those works that I secretly considered good and holy dissolve in the brightness of approaching eternity. . . .

Perhaps we are all like this—unable to perceive anything but our own misery and despairing faint-heartedness in the light of the Beyond that waxes on our horizon.

But it may also be, O Lord, that this sense of being stripped is part of the divine plan. It may be that, in your eyes, our self-satisfaction is the most insolent of our trappings, and that we must present ourselves naked before you so that you, and you alone, may clothe us anew.

Marguerite-Marie Teilhard de Chardin

About this prayer, Father Benedict Groeschel writes in *Stumbling Blocks and Stepping Stones:* "Illness, personal misunderstandings, failure to achieve life goals, and alienation from friends all con-tribute to an abiding sense of sadness. The prayerful person will soon find that this sadness seeks an expression in prayer. Such prayer may not be found in books, nor fit most people's definition of prayer. . . . This prayer of Marguerite Teilhard de Chardin, presi-dent of the Catholic Union of the Sick, and sister of the well-known Jesuit writer, is not without hope, but it is a hope born of pain and suffering. The prayer reminds me that a believer who is not experi-encing sadness at a particular time must appreciate the profound expressions of sadness of others who are enduring severe trials. There must be a special place in purgatory for people who tell the suffering, 'Cheer up. It's not so bad.'"

Job's Lawsuit against God

Questions to Begin

15 minutes
Use a question or two to get warmed up for the reading.

1 Are you the kind of person who
❏ will do almost anything to avoid scenes and keep the peace?
❏ rarely rocks the boat?
❏ prefers to get disagreements out in the open and deal with them?
❏ sometimes likes a good fight to clear the air?
❏ keeps an eye out for opportunities to sue?

2 Describe a situation in which you had to confront someone over a difficult issue. Was the confrontation successful? What did you learn?

3 Describe a situation in which you surprised yourself by saying something you had not meant to say. Was the result fortunate or unfortunate?

5 minutes
Read the passage aloud. Let individuals take turns reading sections.

The Reading: Selections from Job 9; 13; 23; 30

Job Considers a Lawsuit against God

9:2 "[H]ow can a mortal be just before God?
3 If one wished to contend with him,
   one could not answer him once in a thousand.
4 He is wise in heart, and mighty in strength
   —who has resisted him, and succeeded? . . .
14 How then can I answer him,
   choosing my words with him?
15 Though I am innocent, I cannot answer him;
   I must appeal for mercy to my accuser.
16 If I summoned him and he answered me,
   I do not believe that he would listen to my voice.
17 For he crushes me with a tempest,
   and multiplies my wounds without cause;
18 he will not let me get my breath,
   but fills me with bitterness.
19 If it is a contest of strength, he is the strong one!
   If it is a matter of justice, who can summon him?
20 Though I am innocent, my own mouth would condemn me;
   though I am blameless, he would prove me perverse.
21 I am blameless; I do not know myself;
   I loathe my life.
22 It is all one; therefore I say,
   he destroys both the blameless and the wicked.
23 When disaster brings sudden death,
   he mocks at the calamity of the innocent.
24 The earth is given into the hand of the wicked;
   he covers the eyes of its judges—
   if it is not he, who then is it? . . ."

Hope and Despair about a Confrontation with God

13:14 "I will take my flesh in my teeth,
   and put my life in my hand.
15 See, he will kill me; I have no hope;
   but I will defend my ways to his face. . . .

18 I have indeed prepared my case;
      I know that I shall be vindicated. . . .
23 How many are my iniquities and my sins?
      Make me know my transgression and my sin.
24 Why do you hide your face,
      and count me as your enemy? . . .
23:3 Oh, that I knew where I might find him,
      that I might come even to his dwelling!
4 I would lay my case before him,
      and fill my mouth with arguments.
5 I would learn what he would answer me,
      and understand what he would say to me.
6 Would he contend with me in the greatness of his power?
      No; but he would give heed to me.
7 There an upright person could reason with him,
      and I should be acquitted forever by my judge. . . .
12 I have not departed from the commandment of his lips;
      I have treasured in my bosom the words of his mouth.
13 But he stands alone and who can dissuade him?
      What he desires, that he does.
14 For he will complete what he appoints for me;
      and many such things are in his mind.
15 Therefore I am terrified at his presence;
      when I consider, I am in dread of him.
16 God has made my heart faint;
      the Almighty has terrified me;
17 If only I could vanish in darkness,
      and thick darkness would cover my face!"

God Seems Cruel to Job

30:20 "I cry to you and you do not answer me;
      I stand, and you merely look at me.
21 You have turned cruel to me;
      with the might of your hand you persecute me. . . .
25 Did I not weep for those whose day was hard?
      Was not my soul grieved for the poor?
26 But when I looked for good, evil came;
      and when I waited for light, darkness came."

10 minutes
Choose questions according to your interest and time.

1 In these excerpts from his speeches, what does Job seem to want from God?

2 Compare Job's statements about himself and about God in 30:20–21, 25–26. What is Job implying about God?

3 The Satan predicted that Job would curse God, that is, that Job would "charge God with wrongdoing" (1:22). Looking at 9:17 and 9:22–24, would you say that Job does this? Why or why not?

4 Identify Job's expressions of trust in God and confidence in God's justice and also his expressions of terror at God and fear that God is unjust. What picture of God does Job have? Does it make sense?

5 What picture of Job is painted by his statements about God?

A Guide to the Reading

*If participants have not read this section already, read it aloud.
Otherwise go on to "Questions for Application."*

For many chapters, Job and the friends debate the traditional
view that God rewards the just, punishes the wicked, and
rescues the needy (4–31). Job insists that this is not how the
world really is. Look around. Upright people suffer greatly and die
young (24:1–12). People who exploit others prosper, live happy
lives, and go old to their graves, loaded with honors (21:7–15,
23–34). If one is looking for a test case, there is Job himself. If
God dealt with the world as the friends say, Job would not be suffering as he is. The traditional view shatters on the rocks of Job's
innocence (chapter 16).

The friends defend the traditional view without offering any
strikingly new arguments. What they lack in originality, however,
they make up for in vehemence. Eliphaz started out mildly urging
Job to repent while acknowledging Job's integrity (4–5). But as Job
digs in his heels, insists that he has *not* done anything deserving
punishment, and declares that God is dealing with him unjustly, the
friends become hostile and abusive. Faced with Job's intransi-
gence, they slam him with unsupported accusations (22:4–11).

The friends' harshness raises the question whether they
are driven by something besides concern for God's reputation. The
conviction that if you do good God will protect you from earthly
evils provides a feeling of security. By doing good you can, in a
sense, take control of your destiny. Do the friends oppose Job so
strongly because his situation seems to disprove their comforting
theory? Are they terrified at the prospect of facing life without the
guarantee of God's earthly protection and blessing that the traditional view offers?

Because Job is a person of integrity, he will not go through
the motions of repentance when he knows he has not sinned. For
the same reason, he cannot overlook the injustice he sees in the
world. But while Job has discovered that God does not rule the
world with strict justice, he continues to believe that God *ought* to.
Job's outrage at justice violated, revolving around his disappointment with God, pains him more than his grievous losses and physical sickness. It nauseates him to think that the world is an absurd
place where good and evil ultimately make no difference (9:23–26).

44

Job decides to confront God over his failure to execute justice. When the idea of a legal suit against God first occurs to him, Job dismisses it as impossible. God is not the kind of person on whom a marshal can serve papers; God will not submit to a subpoena (9:19). Even if God came to court, Job fears, he would not listen to what Job has to say but would overwhelm Job with questions and countercharges (9:3, 14–16). In any case, in the presence of God, Job would be so frightened that he would blurt out things he didn't intend to say (9:20). Job would end up having to ask his adversary for mercy (9:15).

A further problem in a lawsuit against God is that God would be not only defendant but judge (who else could be?). At moments Job reassures himself that God surely would give a right verdict (13:18; 23:4–11). Job trusts God's justice and faithfulness (23:6–7, 10). But considering the undeserved way that God is treating him (10:5–8), at other moments Job doubts that God would be fair (9:6–18). Job gloomily concludes that no matter how much he was in the right, God would find him guilty (9:28–31).

There seems to be no way to bring God to account for his failure to administer justice. Job's meditations trail off in despair (9:18–22). But his desire for justice will not be suppressed. And so he resumes his attempt, driven on by rage at justice denied (13:14).

In Job's view, God's "job description" includes administering justice in the world. If God lets the wicked prosper and the innocent suffer, he is failing to do his job. A trial between Job and God, then, would have an either/or outcome. Either Job would be shown to be a great sinner, and God was right to have afflicted him so severely. Or Job would be acquitted, and God was wrong to have brought such evils upon him. If Job is vindicated (13:18; 23:7), God will necessarily be found guilty.

God himself has already affirmed that Job *is* innocent. Yet it is inconceivable that God is in the wrong. We are forced to wonder whether this dilemma has any solution.

Questions for Application

40 minutes
Choose questions according to your interest and time.

---

1 In what ways does a person's picture of God have to change and grow as he or she goes through life? How have you experienced this process? What is difficult about it?

---

2 When have you felt that God was treating you or someone else unfairly? Were you angry with God? How did you communicate your thoughts and feelings to him?

---

3 Is it okay to be angry with God? Is it avoidable? When you are angry with God, what should you do or avoid doing? (For reflection: Psalms 13; 74; 88.)

4 In what ways does God seem to execute justice in this world? In what ways does he seem not to?

5 If God does not guarantee that if we do what is right he will protect us against all earthly evils, what does it mean to trust him? How does Jesus' Sermon on the Mount (Matthew 5–7; see especially 5:11–12, 43–48; 6:19–21, 24–34) help to answer this question? How does Jesus' death and resurrection shed light on this question?

"If a question comes up that you can't answer, don't be afraid to admit that you're baffled! Assign the topic as a research project for someone to report on next week."

Fisherman Bible Study Guides

Approach to Prayer

15 minutes
Use this approach—or create your own!

✦ Take a few moments to think about situations of injustice that make you angry (they might be personal or global). Pray Psalm 10 or Psalm 77 as a way of expressing your anger to God and asking him to show his mercy to those who are suffering undeservedly. If you have enough copies of the same translation, pray the psalm together; otherwise, let one person read it aloud for the group. End by praying together an Our Father, a Hail Mary, and a Glory to the Father.

A Living Tradition
Grief and Hope

This section is a supplement for individual reading.

Hope of resurrection had not yet spread widely in Israel at the time the author of Job wrestled with the problem of suffering. But by the time of Jesus most Jews believed in some sort of resurrection, and Jesus gave it a central place in his teaching (Luke 9:23–24; John 12:24–26). Belief in eternal life puts earthly suffering in a new light: we see the possibility that God might use the pains and griefs of the present life to lead us into his eternal kingdom. So the Christian experience of suffering is paradoxical. Anguish and sorrow remain real, yet trust in God's ultimate intentions for us brings us hope, even joy.

This combination of grief and hope is seen in a letter that Jane de Chantal wrote to comfort her daughter Françoise in 1634. In the previous year, Françoise's husband had died on the very day that Françoise gave birth to a son. (With St. Francis de Sales, St. Jane founded the Sisters of the Visitation.)

I was deeply moved by your letter, my darling, which tells me how keenly you are suffering. Truly, your sorrow is great, and, when looked at only in terms of this earthly life, it is overwhelming. But if you can look beyond the ordinary and shifting events of life and consider the infinite blessings and consolations of eternity, you would find comfort in the midst of these reversals, as well as joy in the assured destiny of him for whom you mourn. Oh, when will we learn to be more attentive to these truths of our faith? When will we savor the tenderness of the Divine Will in all the events of our life, seeing in them only His good pleasure and His unchanging, mysterious love, which is always concerned for our good, as much in prosperity as in adversity? But, imperfect as we are, we somehow transform into poison the very medicine the Great Physician prescribes for our healing. Let's stop behaving in such a manner. Rather, like obedient children, let's surrender ourselves lovingly to the will of our heavenly Father and cooperate with his plan to unite us intimately to Himself through suffering. If we do that, He will become all for us: our brother, son, husband, mother, our all in all. Courage! May you find strength in these thoughts.

GOD ENDS THE DEBATE

Questions to Begin

15 minutes
Use a question or two to get warmed up for the reading.

1   What is your favorite animal?
Why?

2   When have you experienced
God's grandeur in nature?
Describe the scene.

5 minutes
Read the passage aloud. Let individuals take turns reading sections.

The Reading: Job 38; 39; 40

God's Turn to Speak

38:1 Then the LORD answered Job out of the whirlwind:
2 "Who is this that darkens counsel by words without
knowledge?
3 Gird up your loins like a man,
I will question you, and you shall declare to me.

4 "Where were you when I laid the foundation of the earth?
Tell me, if you have understanding.
5 Who determined its measurements—surely you know!
Or who stretched the line upon it?
6 On what were its bases sunk,
or who laid its cornerstone
7 when the morning stars sang together
and all the heavenly beings shouted for joy?

8 "Or who shut in the sea with doors
when it burst out from the womb?—
9 when I made the clouds its garment,
and thick darkness its swaddling band,
10 and prescribed bounds for it,
and set bars and doors,
11 and said, 'Thus far shall you come, and no farther,
and here shall your proud waves be stopped'?

12 "Have you commanded the morning since your days began,
and caused the dawn to know its place,
13 so that it might take hold of the skirts of the earth,
and the wicked be shaken out of it?
14 It is changed like clay under the seal,
and it is dyed like a garment.
15 Light is withheld from the wicked,
and their uplifted arm is broken.

¹⁶ "Have you entered into the springs of the sea,
     or walked in the recesses of the deep?
¹⁷ Have the gates of death been revealed to you,
     or have you seen the gates of deep darkness?
¹⁸ Have you comprehended the expanse of the earth?
     Declare, if you know all this.

¹⁹ "Where is the way to the dwelling of light,
     and where is the place of darkness,
²⁰ that you may take it to its territory
     and that you may discern the paths to its home?
²¹ Surely you know, for you were born then,
     and the number of your days is great! . . ."

God Drives the Point Home

³⁹ "Can you hunt the prey for the lion,
     or satisfy the appetite of the young lions,
⁴⁰ when they crouch in their dens,
     or lie in wait in their covert? . . .
^{39:19} Do you give the horse its might?
     Do you clothe its neck with mane?
²⁰ Do you make it leap like the locust?
     Its majestic snorting is terrible. . . .
²⁶ Is it by your wisdom that the hawk soars,
     and spreads its wings toward the south?
²⁷ Is it at your command that the eagle mounts up
     and makes its nest on high? . . ."

Job Gets the Point

^{40:1} And the LORD said to Job:
     ² "Shall a faultfinder contend with the Almighty?
        Anyone who argues with God must respond."
³ Then Job answered the LORD:
     ⁴ "See, I am of small account; what shall I answer you?
        I lay my hand on my mouth.
     ⁵ I have spoken once, and I will not answer;
        twice, but will proceed no further."

10 minutes
Choose questions according to your interest and time.

1 Does God respond directly to the issues that Job and the friends have debated in the readings in Weeks 3 and 4?

2 Why does God ask Job questions rather than make statements to him? What is the point of God's questions to Job?

3 If the book of Job were written today, what questions might God ask Job?

4 Why does God call Job a "faultfinder" (40:2)?

5 In response to God's questions, does Job acknowledge that what he said about God was wrong?

A Guide to the Reading

If participants have not read this section already, read it aloud. Otherwise go on to "Questions for Application."

At the end of the speeches, the friends have not disproved Job's contention that God does not always mete out justice in this world. Job has won the argument. But what advantage is that to him? He has progressed beyond a too-neat view of God and the world. He sees reality more clearly than before. But the reality that he sees makes him bitter (9:18). He declares that he loathes his life. "I do not know myself," he says, meaning, "I am beside myself with rage and despair" (9:21).

To save Job from his bitterness, God appears and speaks to him (chapters 38–41). Surprisingly, however, instead of addressing the issue of divine justice in human society, God asks Job a string of questions about Job's knowledge and control of nature. In effect, God demands to know whether Job has the expertise to function as ruler of the universe. Obviously he does not. Job is not God—which is exactly God's point. As Thomas Aquinas observes, "All these questions are introduced to show that man is not able to attain either divine wisdom or divine power." Because Job is not God, he is in no position to criticize how God runs the world. Job does not have the competence to design a job description for God or to sue God when God fails to meet Job's expectations.

God does not take issue with Job's contention that God allows the wicked to prosper and the just to suffer. God does make a brief reference to judging human beings (38:12–15). But there he does not assert that he executes particular judgment on the wicked. Rather, he poetically describes sending the dawn each day: the daily return of daylight exposes *everyone's* deeds to public view, making crime more difficult (compare 24:15–17). God seems to agree with Job's view that he does not dispense strict justice in this world (so does Jesus, who sees this as God's perfection: Matthew 5:45).

Scholar Robert Gordis suggests that God implies that "just as there is order and harmony in the natural world, though imperfectly grasped by man, so there is order and meaning in the moral sphere, though often incomprehensible to man." Gordis seems right, so long as we emphasize the part about "often incomprehensible to man." God impresses on Job the existence of a mysterious design for the universe (the "counsel" that Job is obscuring—38:2—can also be translated "design"). The design of nature stands as a sign that the creator also has a plan for human beings, and presumably his design for humans is as wise as his design for stars and clouds. But God does not suggest that human beings can penetrate *how* he executes that plan. Far from it!

We might wonder whether God is saying to Job, "How I run the universe is no business of yours." Does God brush aside Job's anguished questions about justice by simply asserting that he is so powerful that he can do whatever he wants? Does God defend himself with the argument that might makes right?

Nowhere in the Bible does God ever dismiss justice as an unimportant issue. It seems that God indicates that Job cannot understand how God chooses to relate to the world because Job lacks divine insight and wisdom. Job's acknowledgment that he cannot argue with God seems to be an implied admission that he cannot grasp the reasons why God deals with his creation as he does (40:4–5).

Another scholar, Norman Whybray, observes that God's questions stress his "loving care for those creatures that can be of no possible *use* to human beings." God emphasizes that nature operates without regard to human interests (38:25–27); large portions of it are quite beyond human control (38:39–41; 39:26–27). God's concerns for the universe are a lot bigger, and stranger, than Job or his friends have recognized. Is the message, then, that humans are too small to be important to God? Is God saying to Job, "I have other fish to fry, and you should accept the fact that your sufferings, no matter how great, can only be of minor concern to the creator of an immense universe"?

It seems clear that God wants Job to realize that the divine plan is too vast for him to comprehend. But if human insignificance were God's message, divine silence would have been a better way to get it across. The simple fact that God *speaks* to Job indicates that Job is enormously important to God.

Questions for Application

40 minutes
Choose questions according to your interest and time.

1 What effect does bitterness have on a person? Does bitterness cloud your relationship with God? What could you do to dispel the cloud?

2 What is the value of having a sense of human smallness in the face of God's greatness?

3 What experiences have helped you recognize your human limitations? Why is it important to know our limitations? Why is it also important to free ourselves from false limits that we might have placed on what we can accomplish? What are some of these false limits?

4 What experiences have helped you trust that God is unfolding a plan for your life even in those times when you cannot grasp what that plan is?

5 If you were Job, at this point in the story would you feel satisfied with the outcome?

6 What is the connection between growing in faith in God and accepting the fact that we can never completely grasp his ways?

"In the sixteen years that our group has been meeting, our attendance has fluctuated between three and eighteen. Some of our best sessions had only three or four people present. Having only a few in attendance has never detracted from what we get out of our group Bible study."

Rena Duff, *Sharing God's Word Today*

Approach to Prayer

15 minutes
Use this approach—or create your own!

✦ Pray together this prayer of John Henry Newman.

God has created me to do him some definite service. . . . I have my mission; I may never know it in this life, but I shall be told it in the next. . . . Therefore I will trust him. Whatever, wherever I am, I can never be thrown away. If I am in sickness, my sickness may serve him; in perplexity, my perplexity may serve him; in sorrow, my sorrow may serve him. My sickness, or perplexity, or sorrow may be necessary causes of some great end, which is quite beyond us. He does nothing in vain; he may prolong my life, he may shorten it; he knows what he is about. He may take away my friends, he may throw me among strangers, he may make me feel desolate, make my spirits sink, hide the future from me— still he knows what he is about.

Living Tradition

Did Job Sin by What He Said about God?

This section is a supplement for individual reading.

T
hrough the centuries, the majority of commentators on the book of Job have concluded that throughout his ordeal "Job did not sin or charge God with wrongdoing" (1:22). Pope Gregory the Great, who lived at the end of the sixth century, believed that the possibility of Job having sinned in speech against God can be ruled out for a couple of reasons:

At the beginning of the book we learned that Satan said to the Lord about Job, "Stretch out your hand and touch him, and see if he does not curse you to your face." In response to this request, blessed Job is permitted to be touched by losses, including the loss of children, by wounds, and by offensive words. The reason, obviously, is that God, who had praised him, was certain that this holy man would never fall into the sin of cursing, as the devil had predicted. Thus whoever finds blessed Job guilty, after his affliction, of sinning in his speech plainly judges the Lord to have been mistaken in his assertion about Job.

It is true that the Lord, in speaking to the devil, displayed Job's present good qualities without guaranteeing that he would continue to do what is right. Nevertheless, it should be known that God would by no means have exposed Job's uprightness to the tempter if he had foreseen that Job would not be able to continue to be upright under the temptation. And so, since the devil was allowed by God to tempt him, whoever judges that he gave way to the temptation accuses the one who allowed it of ignorance.

On the other hand, it is possible to argue that God was well aware that Job would not accept his sufferings but God allowed him to be tested anyway, just as God allowed Adam and Eve—and allows each of us—to be tested, even though he foresees that we will sometimes fail to meet the test. It can also be argued that the outcome of the test of Job *is* an embarrassment for God, because Job does accuse him of acting wrongly (for example, 9:17, 22–24). Nevertheless, at the end of the book, God shows himself less concerned with saving face than with guiding Job and his friends to the truth (38:1–42:9).

Now I Have Seen You

Questions to Begin

15 minutes
Use a question or two to get warmed up for the reading.

---

1 When someone you have disagreed with is proven wrong,
you
❑ usually can't resist saying,
"I told you so!"
❑ keep quiet, but can't hide a
look of triumph.
❑ let someone else know.
❑ help the loser not to lose
face.

---

2 Tell about a situation in which
you discovered that something
you had said or a position you
had taken was mistaken. What
did you do then? Were you
embarrassed?

5 minutes
Read the passage aloud. Let individuals take turns reading sections.

The Reading: Job 40; 42

God Presses Job

40:6 Then the LORD answered Job out of the whirlwind:
7 "Gird up your loins like a man;
I will question you, and you declare to me.
8 Will you even put me in the wrong?
Will you condemn me that you may be justified?
9 Have you an arm like God,
and can you thunder with a voice like his? . . .
15 Look at Behemoth,
which I made just as I made you;
it eats grass like an ox.
16 Its strength is in its loins,
and its power in the muscles of its belly.
17 It makes its tail stiff like a cedar;
the sinews of its thighs are knit together.
18 Its bones are tubes of bronze,
its limbs like bars of iron.
19 It is the first of the great acts of God—
only its Maker can approach it with the sword.
20 For the mountains yield food for it
where all the wild animals play.
21 Under the lotus plants it lies,
in the covert of the reeds and in the marsh.
22 The lotus trees cover it for shade;
the willows of the wadi surround it.
23 Even if the river is turbulent, it is not frightened;
it is confident though Jordan rushes against its mouth.
24 Can one take it with hooks
or pierce its nose with a snare? . . ."

Job Changes His Mind

42:1 Then Job answered the LORD:
2 "I know that you can do all things,
and that no purpose of yours can be thwarted. . . .
3 Therefore I have uttered what I did not understand,

> things too wonderful for me, which I did not
> know. . . .
> 5 I had heard of you by the hearing of the ear,
> but now my eye sees you;
> 6 therefore I despise myself,
> and repent in dust and ashes."

The Friends Are Corrected; Job Is Restored

7 After the LORD had spoken these words to Job, the LORD said to Eliphaz the Temanite: "My wrath is kindled against you and against your two friends; for you have not spoken of me what is right, as my servant Job has. 8 Now therefore take seven bulls and seven rams, and go to my servant Job, and offer up for yourselves a burnt offering; and my servant Job shall pray for you, for I will accept his prayer not to deal with you according to your folly; for you have not spoken of me what is right, as my servant Job has done." 9 So Eliphaz the Temanite and Bildad the Shuhite and Zophar the Naamathite went and did what the LORD had told them; and the LORD accepted Job's prayer.

10 And the LORD restored the fortunes of Job when he had prayed for his friends; and the LORD gave Job twice as much as he had before. 11 Then there came to him all his brothers and sisters and all who had known him before, and they ate bread with him in his house; they showed him sympathy and comforted him for all the evil that the LORD had brought upon him; and each of them gave him a piece of money and a gold ring. 12 The LORD blessed the latter days of Job more than his beginning; and he had fourteen thousand sheep, six thousand camels, a thousand yoke of oxen, and a thousand donkeys. 13 He also had seven sons and three daughters. 14 He named the first Jemimah, the second Keziah, and the third Keren-happuch. 15 In all the land there were no women so beautiful as Job's daughters; and their father gave them an inheritance along with their brothers. 16 After this Job lived one hundred and forty years, and saw his children, and his children's children, four generations. 17 And Job died, old and full of days.

Questions for Careful Reading

10 minutes
Choose questions according to your interest and time.

1 Recall the question about whether Job curses God (page 43, question 3). What do God's words in 40:8 suggest about the answer to this question?

2 Compare 40:8 and 42:7. What does God disapprove of in Job's statements? What does he approve of?

3 By changing his mind (42:1–6) Job returns to his earlier acceptance of God's ways. At the end, we could imagine Job reaffirming what he said in 1:21. But is he different at the end than at the beginning?

4 Does God restore Job's fortunes as a reward for his behavior?

5 Which of Job's original blessings are doubled and which are not? Why? (There is no one right answer.)

6 Job is often referred to as patient. Is he? In what way?

A Guide to the Reading

If participants have not read this section already, read it aloud. Otherwise go on to "Questions for Application."

Job admitted that he was unable to press charges against God, but not that his charges were wrong (40:4–5). Unsatisfied with this response, God continues to confront him (40:7–41:34).

As we have seen, Job believes that God should punish evildoers, reward those who do good, and rescue the oppressed. Yet, inexplicably and maddeningly to Job, God is not administering justice this way. Job himself is a case in point. In Job's thinking, if Job is upright, God has done him an injustice by loading him with suffering. If Job is in the right, God is in the wrong.

God vigorously rejects this reasoning. "Will you condemn me that you may be justified?" God indignantly demands (40:8). Job has reached a wrong conclusion. But where has he gone wrong? God does not disagree with Job's reading of the facts: he does not insist that he *does* execute strict justice in the world or contend that Job *is* a great sinner who deserves to suffer. So the flaw must lie in Job's reasoning about these facts. God does not explain what Job's mistake is; his speech, however, points to it.

God calls Job to consider two mythical creatures that symbolize the forces of destruction in the world. One is Behemoth (which could be translated "The Beast"), the other Leviathan. Behemoth is a kind of super-hippopotamus (40:15–24); Leviathan is an ocean monster (chapter 41). We might think of them as a couple of creatures from the Jurassic Park of the ancient Near Eastern imagination. Only God the creator can control these forces (40:19); Job, as a mere fellow creature, cannot (40:15, 24). Yet if Job does not know how to curb such dangerous beings as Behemoth and Leviathan, how can he claim to know how God ought to bring human wrongdoers under control? How God ought to deal with the evils in the world is not a subject on which Job can speak with any authority.

Thus the flaw in Job's reasoning is revealed. Job insisted that God *ought* to execute strict justice in the world. But Job is in no position to say how God should administer the world. Only the creator of the universe can say how the universe ought to be governed. Job needs to let go of his insistence that God bring justice to the world in ways that suit Job.

This realization leads Job to a straightforward admission that his accusations against God have been unfounded. Job's words in 42:6 might be translated: "Therefore I retract and humbly change my mind." The point is not that Job has come to hate himself but that he rejects his former view.

But what has happened to change Job's outlook? Job already knew that God is the creator and orderer of the universe. He already knew that God's ways are too mysterious for humans to discover (chapter 28). And Job is still suffering sickness and loss (as of 42:2–6, Job's words in 9:17 would still sum up his situation). Moreover God has declined to show him the purpose of his suffering and that of other innocent people. Even though Job acknowledges that God's manner of dealing with his creation is beyond his comprehension, can he be content with this outcome? What now enables Job to let go of his bitterness?

The answer lies in Job's declaration to God: "I had heard of you by the hearing of the ear, but now my eye sees you" (42:5). God has revealed himself to Job. Job is willing to relinquish the administration of justice in the world into the hands of the God that he now knows by personal experience.

God now announces that Job has been right and the friends wrong: God does *not* execute strict justice in the world as Eliphaz and the others maintained, and God is not at all happy with their insistence that he does. God calls their view of him "folly" (42:8), using a form of the same Hebrew word that Job applied to his wife's advice ("foolish," 2:9–10). God does not wish to be loved and trusted simply for bringing earthly well-being—a motivation fostered by the traditional view.

Finally God restores Job's fortunes. His flocks and herds become more numerous than before. God's renewed blessing is best expressed in his lovely daughters, whose names mean, approximately, Dove, Cinnamon Flower, and Box of Eye Shadow. Contrary to custom, Job gives them a share of the inheritance along with their brothers (42:13–15).

Questions for Application

40 minutes
Choose questions according to your interest and time.

1 Why is it important to realize that you cannot figure out God? What experiences have impressed on you the mysteriousness of God's dealings with human beings?

2 Why is God so critical of Eliphaz's view of how God governs the world? How might Eliphaz's view of God distort a person's relationship with God?

3 How might Job experience his restored prosperity differently from his prosperity before his trials? How does suffering change our view of our blessings?

4 Is the ending of the book of Job satisfying? Why or why not?

5 What do you think happened to Job's wife?

6 In your opinion, what is the overall message of the book of Job? What have you gotten out of your reading of Job?

7 How might the book of Job help us in reflecting on sufferings that befall entire groups of people, such as the victims of genocide or epidemic diseases?

"Listening is a difficult skill to cultivate, yet it is also foundational to who we are as God's people."

Jeffrey Arnold, *Seven Tools for Building Effective Groups*

Approach to Prayer

15 minutes
Use this approach—or create your own!

✦ Offer suffering to God, with trust in his mercy. Begin by praying an Our Father together. Then take a few minutes for participants to silently recall those who are in some kind of distress (let anyone who wishes mention particular persons). Then pray together the "Hail, Holy Queen" (on the next page), asking that those who are suffering would come to know "the fruit of her womb, Jesus," in their time of suffering.

A Living Tradition

To You We Send Up Our Sighs

This section is a supplement for individual reading.

The book of Job requires strenuous thinking about God and suffering. But at the end of all our labors to understand, it is right to put the whole matter, and ourselves, in God's hands. One person who had a gift for doing that was a medieval monk named Herman, who belonged to a monastic community in Reichenau, Germany. Herman suffered disabilities that made it impossible for him ever to stand or speak clearly. In his later years he lost his sight. Nevertheless, he enriched the life of the monastery by writing poems and hymns. One prayer of his has become part of the repertoire of many Catholics, who pray it at the end of the rosary or at the end of their night prayers, perhaps before a picture of Jesus and the Blessed Mother. The prayer is commonly known by its Latin title, "Salve, Regina"—"Hail, Holy Queen!"

Blessed Herman made no attempt to deny the pain of human existence. But from the midst of suffering he looked with confidence to the mercy of God, reflected in Our Lady's compassionate face.

> Hail, holy queen,
> mother of mercy
> our life, our sweetness, and our hope!
> To you do we cry,
> poor, banished children of Eve,
> to you do we send up our sighs,
> mourning and weeping
> in this valley of tears.
> Turn, then,
> most gracious advocate,
> your eyes of mercy toward us,
> and after this, our exile,
> show us
> the blessed fruit of your womb,
> Jesus.
> O clement, O loving, O sweet Virgin Mary!
> Pray for us,
> O holy Mother of God,
> that we may be made worthy
> of the promises of Christ.

Jesus and the Meaning of Suffering
Going beyond the Book of Job

The book of Job demolishes a mistaken explanation of human suffering. It refutes the view that God consistently rewards good and punishes evil in this world, and that, accordingly, suffering must be God's punishment of sin, or at least his disciplinary correction. Rather than offering a better explanation, however, the book highlights our human incapacity to master the problem. God impresses on Job his inability to understand, and therefore to criticize, how God rules the world. The suffering that God allows is a mystery we cannot penetrate. The book leaves suffering wrapped in deeper darkness than ever.

Yet suffering is a mystery we cannot stop probing. The problem of pain challenges our faith. Pope John Paul II has remarked that just as the existence of a beautiful, majestic universe opens "the eyes of the human soul to the existence of God," the presence of "evil and suffering seems to obscure this image." For some people, the Pope observes, "the daily drama of so many cases of undeserved suffering and of so many faults without proper punishment" seems to testify to God's nonexistence.

Job, however, is not God's last word on the subject of suffering. God's ultimate word about suffering, as about everything else, is his eternal Word, who became a human being—his Son, born into the world as Jesus of Nazareth. Jesus has put our suffering in a new light, indeed, in an entirely new situation.

The Pope's words quoted above come from a reflection on suffering that he wrote in 1984. In his reflection, entitled *The Christian Meaning of Suffering* (sometimes referred to by its Latin title, *Salvifici Doloris*), John Paul speaks as both theologian and spiritual guide. The Pope's reflections bear the mark of a man who has experienced great suffering. We will conclude this booklet by using John Paul's reflections as a help to viewing suffering in the light of Christ. All the quotations that follow are from his document.

Suffering and death in a new light. In conversation with a Jewish teacher named Nicodemus, Jesus explained that he had come so that men and women might not "perish" but have "eternal life" (John 3:16). Jesus, in other words, came to save us from the ultimate suffering, the suffering that lasts forever—"the loss of eternal life, being rejected by God—damnation."

We are vulnerable to this eternal suffering, and to earthly suffering as well, because of sin. Of course, as is "shown precisely by the example of the just man Job," it is often a mistake to attribute particular sufferings to particular sins. Nevertheless, suffering has its roots in "the sin of the beginnings." In a complex and mysterious way, our susceptibility to suffering and death stems from sin in the sense of estrangement from God—an estrangement that began when the first human beings refused to trust and obey God.

Jesus' mission, then, of saving us from "perishing" was aimed at removing sin, that is, overcoming our estrangement from God. Quite simply, Jesus accomplished his mission by dying and rising from the dead. He "conquers sin by his obedience unto death, and he overcomes death by his resurrection."

Jesus' death and resurrection have not ended suffering but have put it in a new light. First, Jesus "blots out from human history the dominion of sin" and gives us "the possibility of living in sanctifying grace." This means that we can escape the fate of wasting our lives. With God's forgiveness and help, the evils that befall us cannot prevent us from becoming the holy men and women that God intends us to be.

Second, Jesus "takes away the dominion of death, by his resurrection beginning the process of the future resurrection of the body." Thus, suffering and death no longer mean the end of us. We are destined not to perish eternally but to live with God forever. In Jesus' resurrection we find "a completely new light," which helps us go forward through the darkness of suffering and humiliations, doubts and hopelessness.

We might say that Jesus' death and resurrection have taken our suffering out of the frame of despair and put it into the frame of hope—hope for holiness and for eternal life. But more than that, Jesus has changed the picture inside the frame, for he has changed our suffering by entering into it.

Suffering welded to love. The Pope points out that Jesus' death was both the world's greatest expression of love and the experience of the most profound suffering. Jesus' prayer in the garden of Gethsemane before his arrest ("My Father, if it is possible, let this cup pass from me; yet not what I want but what you want," Matthew 26:39) demonstrated his love for the Father. And, the Pope reasons, if suffering is measured by the greatness of the evil suffered, Jesus' suffering was unsurpassed, since on the cross he bore the weight of all human sin. On the cross Jesus suffered much more than physical pain. As his cry from the cross shows ("My God, my God, why have you forsaken me?" Mark 15:34), Jesus experienced utter desolation. The Father "laid on him the iniquity of us all" (Isaiah 53:6). Jesus was crushed under a "horrible weight, encompassing the 'entire' evil of the turning away from God which is contained in sin." He endured "in a humanly inexpressible way this suffering which is the separation, the rejection by the Father, the estrangement from God." He descended into the depths of human physical and spiritual pain.

In Jesus' suffering, the Pope explains, "sins are canceled out precisely because he alone, as the only-begotten Son, could take them upon himself, and accept them with that love for the Father which overcomes the evil of every sin." By suffering human estrangement from God out of love for God, Jesus overcomes the estrangement. Human alienation from God was swallowed up in something greater—the Son's love for the Father. "In a certain sense," John Paul writes, Jesus "annihilates this evil in the spiritual space of the relationship between God and humanity, and fills this space with good."

Thus on Golgotha, love and suffering were combined in an utterly unique way. "Human suffering has reached its culmination in the passion of Christ," the Pope explains, "and at the same time it . . . has been linked to love, to that love . . . which creates good, drawing it out by means of suffering." Consequently, Jesus' suffering not only bridges the chasm that had opened between God and humanity, it changes suffering itself by making it the instrument of redemption. We might say that by entering into human suffering with divine love, Jesus has made suffering the location of a divine-human exchange.

John Paul believes that each human being has his or her
own share not only in the *effects* of the redemption but also in the
suffering that has brought it about. Because the Son of God "in his
redemptive suffering has become, in a certain sense, a sharer in
all human sufferings," each human being, in his or her suffering,
"is also called to share in that suffering through which the redemption was accomplished." We can discover "Jesus present in our
sufferings" and, as we do, he can raise us up through our suffering
into the life of God, just as he has passed through his suffering into
God's presence.

Jesus died in a condition of abject human weakness. "This
means that the weaknesses of all human sufferings are capable of
being infused with the same power of God manifested in Christ's
cross." Thus "to suffer means to become . . . particularly open to
the working of the salvific powers of God, offered to humanity in
Christ." At Golgotha God showed that he "wishes to make his power
known precisely through . . . weakness and emptying of self."

St. Paul touched on this subject when he said: "In my
flesh I am completing what is lacking in Christ's afflictions for the
sake of his body, that is, the church" (Colossians 1:24). This is a
mysterious statement, which John Paul explains this way: "The
sufferings of Christ created the good of the world's redemption.
This good in itself is inexhaustible and infinite. No man can add
anything to it. But at the same time, in the mystery of the Church
as his Body, Christ has in a sense opened his own redemptive
suffering to all human suffering. Insofar as man becomes a sharer
in Christ's sufferings in any part of the world and at any time in
history, to that extent he in his own way completes the suffering
through which Christ accomplished the redemption of the world."

"Come, follow me." At times the primary recipient of
God's action through suffering is the sufferer himself or herself.
The Pope points out that suffering often plays a crucial role in the
process by which we become aware of God and begin to seek him
wholeheartedly. "In suffering there is concealed a particular power
that draws a person interiorly close to Christ, a special grace. To
this grace many saints, such as St. Francis of Assisi, St. Ignatius

of Loyola, and others, owe their profound conversion." Both Francis and Ignatius experienced a conversion to God while recovering from injuries.

As an experienced pastor, the Holy Father recognizes that the process by which suffering leads to "interior maturity and spiritual greatness" does not depend primarily on our own willpower but on Christ. "It is he himself who acts at the heart of human sufferings through his Spirit. . . . It is he, as the interior Master and Guide, who reveals to the suffering brother and sister this wonderful interchange, situated at the very heart of the mystery of the Redemption."

The process is a matter of responding to Jesus. "People react to suffering in different ways," the Holy Father observes. "But in general it can be said that almost always the individual enters suffering with a typically human protest and with the question 'why.' . . . He cannot help noticing that the One to whom he puts the question is Himself suffering and wishes to answer him from the cross, from the heart of His own suffering. Nevertheless, it often takes time, even a long time, for this answer to begin to be interiorly perceived. . . . Christ does not explain in the abstract the reasons for suffering, but before all else he says: 'Follow me!' Come! Take part through your suffering in this work of saving the world, a salvation achieved through my suffering! Through my cross! Gradually, as the individual takes up his cross, spiritually uniting himself to the cross of Christ, the salvific meaning of suffering is revealed before him."

Thus, John Paul believes, there is the possibility of joy even in the deepest pain. The Pope points out that often the suffering person "feels condemned to receive help and assistance from others, and at the same time seems useless." But "the discovery of the salvific meaning of suffering in union with Christ transforms this depressing feeling. Faith in sharing in the suffering of Christ brings with it the interior certainty that . . . in the spiritual dimension of the work of redemption," the suffering person "is serving, like Christ, the salvation of his brothers and sisters." Indeed, the person who unites his or her sufferings with those of Christ "is carrying out an irreplaceable service." For suffering, "more than anything else, makes present in the history of humanity the powers of the Redemption. . . . The springs of divine power gush forth precisely in the midst of human weakness. Those who share in the sufferings of Christ preserve in their own sufferings a very special particle of the infinite treasure of the world's Redemption, and can share this treasure with others."

None of this means that suffering itself is good, to be sought for its own sake. "Suffering is, in itself, an experience of evil," the Pope declares. "But Christ has made suffering the firmest basis of the definitive good, namely the good of eternal salvation. By his suffering on the cross, Christ reached the very roots of evil."

Suffering unleashes love. While Jesus invites us to unite our own sufferings with his, he invites us also to unite with him in relieving the suffering of others. The great image of this call, the Pope writes, is the good Samaritan, who feels compassion for an injured man and gives himself generously to helping the injured one (Luke 10:25–37). "This parable witnesses to the fact that Christ's revelation of the salvific meaning of suffering is in no way identified with an attitude of passivity. . . . The Gospel is the negation of passivity in the face of suffering." Jesus showed his active compassion by healing people who were sick or disabled. God allows suffering not only because he wishes to work through it, but also "in order to unleash love in the human person," John Paul declares, "in order to give birth to works of love towards neighbor."

Thus there are two complementary purposes of suffering. Suffering is the opportunity to share in the sufferings of Christ in order to advance God's redemptive activity in the world. Suffering is also a spur to love, provoking us to actively demonstrate God's care for our neighbors. "Christ has taught man to do good by his suffering and to do good to those who suffer," John Paul concludes. Both purposes of suffering call us to cooperate with God's grace and become channels of God's love.

Suggestions for Bible Discussion Groups

Like a camping trip, a Bible discussion group works best if you agree on what you're undertaking together, why you're doing it, where you hope to get to, and how you intend to get there. Many groups use their first meeting to consider such questions. Here is a checklist of issues, with a few bits of advice from people with experience in Bible discussions. (A planning discussion will go more smoothly if the leaders have thought through the following issues beforehand.)

Agree on your purpose. Are you getting together to gain wisdom and direction for your life? to finally get acquainted with the Bible? to support one another in following Christ? to encourage those who are exploring—or reexploring—the Church? for other reasons?

Agree on attitudes. For example: "We're all beginners here." "We're here to help each other understand and respond to God's Word." "We're not here to offer counseling or direction to each other." "We want to read Scripture prayerfully." What do *you* wish to emphasize? Make it explicit!

Agree on ground rules. Barbara J. Fleischer, in her useful book *Facilitating for Growth,* recommends that a group clearly state its approach to the following:

+ Preparation. Do we agree to read the material before each meeting?

+ Attendance. What kind of priority will we give to our meetings?

+ Self-revelation. Are we willing to gradually help the others in the group get to know us—our weaknesses as well as our strengths, our needs as well as our gifts?

+ Listening. Will we commit ourselves to listen to each other?

+ Confidentiality. Will we keep everything that is shared with the group in the group?

+ Encouragement and support. Will we give as well as receive?

+ Participation. Will we work to allow everyone time and opportunity to make a contribution?

You could probably take a pen and draw a circle around listening and confidentiality. Those two points are especially important.

The following items could be added to Fleischer's list:

+ Relationship with parish. Is our group part of the religious education program? independent but operating with the express approval of the pastor? not a parish-based group at all?

+ New members. In the course of the six meetings, will new members be allowed?

Agree on timing and housekeeping.

+ When will we meet?

+ How often will we meet? Weekly or every other week is best if you can manage it. William Riley remarks, "Meetings once a month are too distant from each other for the threads of the last session not to be lost" (*The Bible Study Group: An Owner's Manual*).

+ How long will meetings run?

+ Where will we meet?

+ Is any setup needed? Christine Dodd writes that "the problem with meeting in a place like a church hall is that it can be very soul-destroying" given the cold, impersonal feel of many church facilities. If you have to meet in a church facility, Dodd recommends doing something to make the area homey (*Making Scripture Work*).

+ Who will host the meetings? Leaders and hosts are not necessarily identical.

+ Will we have refreshments? Who will provide them?

+ What about child care? Most experienced leaders of Bible discussion groups discourage bringing infants or other children to adult Bible discussions.

Agree on leadership. You need someone to facilitate—to keep the discussion on track, to see that everyone has a chance to speak, to help the group stay on schedule. Rena Duff, editor of the newsletter *Sharing God's Word Today,* recommends having two or three people take turns leading the discussions.

It's okay if the leader is not an expert regarding the Bible. You have this booklet, and if questions come up that no one can answer, you can delegate a participant to do a little research between meetings. It's important for the leader to set an example of listening, to draw out the quieter members (and occasionally restrain the more vocal ones), to move the group on when it gets stuck, to remind the members of their agreements, and to summarize what the group is accomplishing.

Bible discussion is an opportunity to experience the fulfillment of Jesus' promise "Where two or three are gathered in my name, I am there among them" (Matthew 18:20). Put your discussion group in Jesus' hands. Pray for the guidance of the Spirit. And have a great time exploring God's Word together!

Suggestions for Individuals

Y ou can use this booklet just as well for individual study as for group discussion. While discussing the Bible with other people can be a rich experience, there are advantages to individual reading. For example:

✦ You can focus on the points that interest you most.

✦ You can go at your own pace.

✦ You can be completely relaxed and unashamedly honest in your answers to all the questions, since you don't have to share them with anyone else!

My suggestions for using this booklet on your own are these:

✦ Don't skip "Questions to Begin." The questions can help you as an individual reader warm up to the topic of the reading.

✦ Take your time on "Questions for Careful Reading" and "Questions for Application." While a group will probably not have enough time to work on all the questions, you can allow yourself the time to consider all of them if you are using the booklet by yourself.

✦ If you are going through Job at your own pace, consider reading the entire book, not just the parts excerpted in this booklet. A study Bible (a version with notes) or a commentary would give you some guidance in reading the additional portions. See page 80 for suggested resources.

✦ Since you control the pace, give yourself plenty of opportunities to reflect on the meaning of Job for you. Let your reading be an opportunity for the book of Job to become God's words to you.

Bibles

The following editions of the Bible contain the full set of biblical books recognized by the Catholic Church, along with a great deal of useful explanatory material:

+ The Catholic Study Bible (Oxford University Press), which uses the text of the New American Bible

+ The Catholic Bible: Personal Study Edition (Oxford University Press), which also uses the text of the New American Bible

+ The New Jerusalem Bible, the regular (not the standard or reader's) edition (Doubleday)

Books

+ Michael D. Guinan, *Job,* Collegeville Bible Commentary (Collegeville, Minnesota: Liturgical Press, 1986).

+ Roland E. Murphy, *The Psalms, Job,* Proclamation Commentaries (Philadelphia: Fortress Press, 1977).

+ Norman C. Habel, *The Book of Job,* The Old Testament Library (Philadelphia: Westminster Press, 1985).

+ Robert Gordis, *The Book of God and Man: A Study of Job* (Chicago: University of Chicago Press, 1965).

How has Scripture had an impact on your life? Was this booklet helpful to you in your study of the Bible? Please send comments, suggestions, and personal experiences to Kevin Perrotta c/o Trade Editorial Department, Loyola Press, 3441 N. Ashland Ave., Chicago, IL 60657.